Mono No Aware

poems by

Matt Prater

Finishing Line Press
Georgetown, Kentucky

Mono No Aware

Copyright © 2016 by Matt Prater
ISBN 978-1-62229-980-5 First Edition
All rights reserved under International and Pan-American Copyright Conventions.
No part of this book may be reproduced in any manner whatsoever without written permission from the publisher, except in the case of brief quotations embodied in critical articles and reviews.

ACKNOWLEDGMENTS

The author would like to thank the following publications, where some of the pieces in this volume have appeared (or are forthcoming), sometimes in different form:

Appalachian Heritage – "God's Work"
Floyd County Moonshine – "The Painted Saw"
James Dickey Review – "The Music, East Tennessee"
Motif – "Mono No Aware"
Now & Then: The Appalachian Magazine – "A Genealogy"
Still: The Journal – "A School for the Magical Arts"

Editor: Christen Kincaid

Cover Photo: Matt Prater

Author Photo: Matt Prater

Cover Design: Elizabeth Maines

Printed in the USA on acid-free paper.
Order online: www.finishinglinepress.com
also available on amazon.com

Author inquiries and mail orders:
Finishing Line Press
P. O. Box 1626
Georgetown, Kentucky 40324
U. S. A.

Table of Contents

Mono No Aware: 1

Appalachian: Open Letter: 8

A School for the Magical Arts: 9

A Genealogy: 10

Jerusalem Artichoke: 11

Flying Shoes: 12

The Music, East Tennessee: 13

The Painted Saw: 15

God's Work: 17

Snow Job: 19

Meditation at the Great Channels: 21

Mono No Aware
—for Cathy Smith Bowers

I   The people have no history.
We live in myths. Our
dreams are sacred texts
from more than air.

We poets are, re Walcott,
conspicuous creatures of morning.
Except when Southern. Us Southern poets,
as you said someone said,

are always telling the stories, always,
of someone loved, invariably
dead, from an amalgamation
of little blistered heroes,

all of them dead,
whose misdemeanory
and dense uncensored howl
thumps out God's heart.

Everyone has felt more pain than us,
who, moaning in our menses
and malaise, just come across as
tacky, middle class.

And yet the need remains
to tell ourselves about ourselves,
about our neighbors,
about the mottled world

of desk clerks
and high school janitors
playing hanky panky
and Jack Rocks

in the Home Ec room
linen closet. And all of these
fuzzy dreamstones,
as you might call them,

make new poems old
and form the mythos of our lives.
This is what Miller meant, I think,
by *old wine in new bottles*.

And so we line out song
from scraps of song,
which can not quite define
and can't last long.

II All wise beings have
ambiguous beginnings. Stone
has hot and virile
in its youth.

Withered things,
sublime trees, storytellers,
lived with suspect elements
and got around.

A tree without a seed
burst open. Paw-Paw ate,
and fished beside
a stream original.

God made the fish, men
dug the lake, then
put God's fish inside
to take them out.

Now don't ask me
whether God and men
agreed that this was good,
or where any of the fish stood.

I only know that my friend had a boss
whose daddy owned the lake
and that he let my friend
go out there fishing,

and let my friend let me
come on as well, to tag along
and drive
and steal his spinners.

The lake was called Lost Lake,
in Grayson County,
where everything is green
and almost good.

We went one summer
more than once or twice,
and caught enough
to fill five frying pans.

There was an old boat on the dock
we would take out, casting
into every marsh till there was
lavender below the moon.

Wayward herons
stared out from the locusts
as we cast our lines
and nets into the marsh.

The boat got caught
on old stumps once or twice,
and every evening herons
failed to strike.

We waited till the sky washed orangepink,
and the gibbous, like a fish eye,
pointed home. Then we pushed out
into coffee the lake was then,

and the heron finally dove into the marsh
and took a largemouth
I'd been feeding meal worms
for an hour.

III   One night (a full moon, graciously),
when we got to my car I'd locked us out.
We had to walk, guarded by moonlight, until
an Ivy League professor picked us up.

He asked us who we were. We said
from Saltville. He asked us what we did.
We told him school. He asked me
what I studied: Appalachia.

Hearing that he talked a lot
about the dead, who never had much
and were proud of that. That he
had met them, though now

they were gone. All of them. All.
The woman who ate early, in the dark,
and didn't like to speak much,
he knew her well. Now

she was dead. And none left alive
was of that mold. They liked to work,
were stoic, rustic, built. And all were dead.
He knew them, once, almost.

He had remained to tidy up the graves,
and because all intellectuals, or at least those
who have made congress with the dead,
revere their own Romantical exile.

He wanted to retire eccentrically.
His wife had been a chair professor, too.
He drove a Land Rover, or something like it.
His other boots were muddy at the door.

Their house was more than nice.
Their land was better: cattle nibbled broomsedge
near the driveway, and more stars
than Orion's met the eye.

The house they had was everything
I'd wanted: mud on the doorstep
and a big library, and green herbs
drying over rafters in the air.

They sat us on the couch, they gave us water,
and let us use the phone to call my house.
The wife asked if we'd like to watch television.
We didn't. So we talked about the dead.

Then he asked why I studied Appalachia.
I couldn't tell him why. He said *that figures*,
one of many things his wife
almost chided him for.

My friend, mostly, said nothing.
He knew that he was very much alive.
He knew the air of anthropology. And he
was not enamored by insults.

We were another errand, obligation,
one more trip, just another doublewide,
where the lights were out
and the world was always dying.

IV   My uncle used to go to Tennessee.
He had a 5th wheel camper
at an old folks' RV home, a warm porch
in a quiet neighborhood.

We would sit out with mosquitoes
while he listened to the sky
and talked about some rivers
that we never fished,

or talk about some shooting
we would never do,
or not talk about the war
he didn't win, or

that the mountains there
looked like mountains here.
Sometimes he'd pull things
out of closets for me,

and I'd be shocked by
a heavy Swiss fishing reel
or some lead bodied fly lures
in a real rabbit fur pouch.

I carry a lost pocket knife
wherever I go. It's usable and sharp
and dangerous, full of a boy's
longing for sex and fire.

My uncle gave it to me
in great economy.
My mother didn't like it,
but it stayed.

It could open a fish
like the fish opened water,
except that when the gullet fell
it didn't close or bubble.

I don't know where I lost the knife;
I did. But losing it diminishes
exactly nothing. My uncle's gift
was mostly ceremony:

a hope of his that I would carry
something, a love for the dilapidated world,
for piping insulation, stripping floors,
for hunting grouse and throwing square bales home.

So I look at things I've never used. A lot.
Jars that once held dandelion wine
rest empty but ghostscented on our walls, in the house
of three schoolteachers and their specters.

V   Mono no aware,
in rough translation,
describes "wistful acceptance"
of death and loss.

Fall's orange ochre:
mono no aware. The tears
boys cry on football
senior night.

It's still 1982
on state route 469,
still 60 cents for a gallon of gas
on an RC Cola sign.

In towns between the curves
of almost estuaries, my car is palmed
by slaps of straggled hay
and chicory.

Each mile or so
the tatters of a Gothic revival
pop out from mats
of locust and wisteria.

Across a bridge across a stream across the road,
in the wake of a rustwheeled singlewide,
hayscented fern grows
through the rot of a wicker chair.

God made night first;
remember that. The moon
is dripping
firefly medicine.

Appalachian: Open Letter

We are not only granny's cooking pot, a reflection
in the oneiric cistern, or bee balm on a mountain glade,
the memory of bottle Coke with Daddy at a dinosaured Esso station;
we are also the things that burn, the things that *smart*:
a word that indicates a way of wisdom,
if we only knew what to do with the information.

Forget the ache which, beyond logic, pulls us back if we leave the hills.
Forget the public image, if not the image we have of ourselves.
Forget the consolations of wisteria,
the hammer dulcimer and farrier's hammer.
Forget the farm you did not grow up on,
and just answer me this:

what do you do when you already know where home is,
if you've never doubted that at all,
if you didn't need to be an exile in the Rust Belt,
or lose the farm or buy it, to figure out
that your life is entangled in a particular us?
What if knowing that isn't enough?

A School for the Magical Arts

What disappeared with her was that this locust,
the fifteenth from the rusted scarlet cattle gates
on Bonita Serra Road, entrance to the Collins' farm,
was the best place on the property to hang up
bird and squirrel feeders. Next to the greeny
fungused fence posts were telephone wires
and escape routes from the switchbacked curvy road;
other branches hung across the curves, too –
byways against the plod of F250s. She was a woman
who still ate souse, who still made souse, crazy
quilted blankets from old t-shirts and broken jeans,
and overlooked all sins until the age of twelve.
She hated Harry Potter, owned no television,
and was a one-woman school in the magical arts.
She never would have admitted that; moreover,
that she wasn't ignorant of the fact herself.
She was a Christian witch, and held no contradiction
between the Levitical injunctions against sorcery
and the skills she commanded in natural potency.
For what is magic but traditional chemical knowledge,
interpretation of strange sights, communication
across seemingly impossible strands, and intimacy
with codes of healing God has planted in the earth?
Forget trigrams and crystals, and the avatars
of what hides behind the avatars; real wizardry
is a boiling pot of chicory, moon planting skills,
and knowledge of what a warbler's movement holds.
It is not what the snake offered, and is not always a sight
of excitement. The real thing is always only medicine;
in fact, to those who practice it, that word's preferred.
Some women are given tongues of angels, prophecies,
and heal through God's own hand with empty hands.
Some others understand the tongues of red tails,
make poultices and cancer-killing teas. Jesus himself
once used spit and dirt to heal; and God was pleased.
So who's to say which one contains more blessing:
the angel's stirring hand, or the stirred up well?

A Genealogy

From the first of them to come out of Pennsylvania
to the last of them to curse in German
when her children made her angry,
there were three generations.

And from the first of them to speak only English
to the first of them to work outside the home,
taking chopped Confederate bones to the blessing heap,
there were three generations more.

And from that first Eleord nurse, to the first
Eleord girl to work at Matheson,
building bombs to heap out German eyes,
there were three generations still.

Twenty years later, Mrs. Eleord
tells her husband "it made sense for you men
to eat your dinner first
back when you all had jobs."

Twenty years after that, Ms. Eleord
tells her daughter, "if Bird Dog Stephenson
gets that job over you, you will
sue this county for everything it's worth."

And now, fourteen generations on, Kasey Eleord
drives around the bend in her new red crew cab Ford. She
picks up her new boyfriend for their date,
and doesn't slide to shotgun when he climbs in.

Jerusalem Artichoke

In this country of counties of lack,
tangles of mint sprigs line the ambling,
diversion borne creeks below old
half-restored grist mills,

and edible funk is bursting
from the untreated mast at the edges
of abandoned farms. The world
is a teeming sultry angel

whose number I used to have here
somewhere, folded in a wallet
on a lipstick smudged
or Stetson scented napkin.

But I can't remember names
anymore, or whether the earth was
a man or a woman, or both. What type
of mint I smell now I don't know.

For all I know, each thing could be
a poison angel mushroom. If I am as lost
in my own native corn as a traveler
in some distant foreign city,

where the names of plants
are the only necessary annals,
I have not earned the right to taste
the brooding sacrificial wings

of the elderberry or the wild mint,
or the nettle or the tart yellow sorrel,
or the hickory, or the goatsbeard,
or the tall Jerusalem artichoke,

these names I know and recite
like Proust or the dense Nietzsche,
whose words I would only recognize
in passing flashes along the way.

Flying Shoes

I'm at a mountain lookout
on a full moon evening. Storms
are sliding along the valley's other side.
I'm not sure where I'm going,

but the bottom of the moon
is almost pink beside pink bottomed
clouds, and the breeze is slow
and wet and pleasant,

and these movements are slow
enough to contemplate. Shifting
winds may bring isolated
storms tonight, the radio says

between "Lady Down on Love"
and "Daddy Never Was The Cadillac Kind".
It's Sunday night, and Randy Owen
is spinning those fine old songs

that are not one bit as simple
as I might've used to think, or say.
Whenever I throw *The Book of Changes*,
and the pattern and the shift

is brought up to me, and I see that
it's time to loosen some dependency,
to cherish then let go
in the words of my translation,

is that not the same as when,
aimlessly poking the radio scanner
along the curves of NC 421,
"Just To See You Smile"

comes on, then, rounding into
Mountain City, not "Copperhead Road"
as one might be given to think, but
a college DJ spinning "Tennessee Blues."

The Music, East Tennessee

I loved it all: pitch and timber sticking in my fingers,
                a barrel of biscuits
                      stuck to the tips of my teeth. Shaking
off molasses with the cat of my tongue, bumbling along

with you to God knows where. We had this redone black
                '75 Ford pickup (except
                      it had got undone again,
just like us). We were heading to the First Jesus Church

of Mountain Home. I didn't know any hymns, but
                you said you'd been there
                before, and none of ladies
could hear much anymore, so if I just kind of hummed

a bit, no one would notice. Besides, they were paying us
                in cobbler pie and gravy steaks,
                so I was good to go.
I'd lost my driver's license in a card game (the guy I played

looked just like me, but he was only nineteen then,
                and wanted liquor),
                so you were driving.
And damn, if you drove for shit. Couldn't go one mile

without dragging on the rumble strip for half. And our guitars
                had to be in the cab,
                since it was raining, so I got stuck
holding out for three hours in a pisspour with a two dollar poncho

trying to ride that epileptic horse of a truck bed. To beat it all
                when we got there,
                they'd changed theologies on us:
no guitars anymore. And it threw me off for everything, and man

if I bombed. By the time we were done with two songs
                I heard somebody whisper
                something about two long-toothed drunks,
and as soon as we were done, and the blessing'd been said

for the food, this old man walked us and asked me
                if I was assured of my salvation.
                And I told him yes, sir, I'm sure,
but I told you I'm sure gonna kick your ass if you don't

get me outta here in fifteen minutes. But I ain't
                ate dessert yet, you said.
                We're going to fucking Denny's.
And so we did, and so it was just one more busted night

in that life of busts and hot licks we lived for fifteen years.
                Sometimes it was high and tight
                for months, singing
like kestrel birds, eating brisket and bacon. And sometimes

you were pouting in the lobby of Denny's because you
                hadn't got your cobbler,
                and I was pouting cause
some old man called me a heathen, and was right.

The Painted Saw

When my great granny Suzie Troxell died,
we cleaned her house of some hundred hundred
playthings. My aunt took a Round Tuit,
while Daddy got his Paw Paw's final box
of Tampa Nugget Sublime cigars.
He had asked for a handsaw, too,
to keep around for daily use. But Granny
said the four of them that were left
would be split up between the family,
oiled up and repainted. He'd get one
but he'd have to wait for it. He thought
she meant she'd have the handle varnished,
rust took off so the saw would keep for work;
so of course he was fine with that. But then
some Sundays later, Granny came by after church
with the saw wrapped up in a towel
in the back of her car. You might not like
what I had done with it, she warned him
as he opened the refurbished thing,
now part of some scattered altarpiece.
By painted she'd meant artwork,
galloping deer in a mast of locust leaves.
The work done wasn't bad, to tell the truth:
each saw held a season, and all were of a piece,
so that the four together told a longer story.
The only problem was that story wasn't work.
He has a sentiment for action over object;
the competence of used things holds the dead,
and when used up the use stays on with us.
The way I think he sees it, ghosts should move.
So we all knew he didn't like it; but he lied,
said it was real nice, and hung it on the mantle.
Then complained about it, mumbling, for a week,
until my mother set him to a little carpentry.
The wrought iron fence that lined our porch,
and which had done that since her Daddy
had put it up her whole lifetime ago, had aged
so much the columns now whistled in storms
through rust holes lined out unstrategically
along each section. With a few more years
the whole thing might have given way,
so though she hated losing anything, made
Daddy find a way to fix it and lose nothing.

My mother has a different sense of spirits:
the world is filled with traces of the holy,
and essences of hosts can hide in things.
The soul lives on without the body, yes;
but sometimes it is nice to touch that chair,
that pot, that spoon or cloth they used;
preserving these things keeps the users linked.
So what my father did was break the columns,
replacing them with precut cedar posts. But he kept
the iron fence rows, which now bore nothing,
bolting them as decorations between the posts.
By this, the fence's use and story both continued,
he got to work and she stayed in connection.
But what was best in all in this was that
during this process, having been sent out
to get masonry screws at the store, I came back
to find him cutting posts with a painted saw,
a herd of deer dancing deep inside the wood.

God's Work

Blaze had run a septic cleaning company
for fifteen years, called Blaze's Sewer Review.
His emblem? Dead skunk in a crosshairs
above the motto Dirty deeds done dirt cheap!
His only son, name Cody, had almost finished
his Associate's in maybe becoming a teacher or a cop,
but now was taking an accidental gap year
where he'd forgot to renew his grants (and made two Ds).
Blaze pretended to be displeased, but truth be told
was happy to have his son around again.
Cody had lived at his mother's house
for almost all of high school, since Blaze
had kept his place outside the good school district.
So Blaze moved back from the hose to the truck cab,
and Cody went to vacuuming up poop, taking back
his sixteenth summer's work for his twenty-first.
The sun was hot and the shit stank
and the pay was never low but it wasn't high
and only certain kinds of women didn't mind
a man who had that station of employment.
But the two made a tolerable living,
and knew where to find those women.
But then that Glade tornado came and tore Glade up.
If nobody had died, it'd have been something to gloat about:
two square miles of short circuited crap bombs
and them sitting right there, rolling in it (so to speak).
But people did die, and others wished they had,
and more than that lost Mommy's house and all her things.
The trees looked like the hair line in a razor ad.
So they didn't like the work they took,
and took some cheap, for dinner or beer.
Sometimes they had to do stump removal,
or spend a half day moving furniture
before they got to shoveling out the tank.
They didn't put that on the bill. Almost all
they got paid full for was Jobsite Johnny cleanup,
and it seemed to rain about half of the festivals out.
But nothing was worse than when that church group came
to take the trash and trees from Gladys Lamie's yard.
Jerusalem Church of Jesus the Servant youth group:
twenty-five neon t-shirts strong from St. Jean-Baptiste, Iowa.
Every one picking up trash with one hand, cell phones
in the other; every one mixing up the names of tools,

asking folks about their accents, not getting jack shit done.
Mrs. Lamie'd double-booked the day; so Blaze and Cody
had to watch all this and try to work around it.
Everything done something they could have done in half the time
without the trouble, everything not done something
keeping them from getting to their work.
But the kids were doing God's work, Gladys said;
she held their hands then cried as they prayed for her.
So Blaze and Cody kept their mouths shut for a while
But before the kids were halfway done cleaning
they'd stopped for lunch and pictures.
The girls duckfaced in Jesus name,
with those matching neon shirts: big heart in a house
read Spreading His love to the whole world!
Preacher's lady clicked that Nikon camera
while the girls duckfaced and the boys got a chainsaw
stuck in a stump, and flooded out the engine.
Finally it all just ate Blaze up too much.
'If a man came in on that stump at angles
he wouldn't have that problem,' he hinted to the boys.
'Do ya'll want it I could get that out for you?'
'We're sorry, sir, but we can't let you do that,'
the preacher said. 'You have to be approved to volunteer.'
'Ah, I think we know how to work with tools.'
'Well all the same, we best get this alone.'
And that was all the two said to each other.
The preacher preached and the shovelers shoveled
and neither spoke to the other one again.
But later, heading home, Blaze turned to Cody
and said 'My daddy only ever told me one thing
about religion: 'You do God's work, but never call it that.'
And that's the only thing I'm going to say to you.'

Snow Job

"Captain, captive / of your fate..."
    —*Samuel Menashe*

There's an episode of King of the Hill, "Snow Job,"
where Buck gets flustered over a boobie calendar,
has a heart attack, and almost dies. By this point
Hank has worked at Strickland Propane fifteen years,
but gets passed up for manager by a lackey with an MBA.
When the new boss decides to jack up prices in cold weather,
Hank, distraught, packs up the family and sabbaticals to the lake
where, amazed by the kindness of a teller at a roadside store,
he sees the great epiphany of a new career in general goods.
This reminds me of a certain saint, it need not be Augustine,
who, recovering from injuries, sat in contemplation
over just which kind of good life he should leave.
For a while he basked in the pleasures of knight errantry,
and considered the gangrenous root a kind of pleasure as well.
So long as he thought on the thought, the thought felt well.
Still, after feeling for a while he did then not feel,
and whenever his imagination tired of dragons,
the bruised root swelled. Malaise and diarrhea were his lot.
But at times there was another contemplation.
Some young boy who had never had a penny candy
or a father or the knowledge of salvation
would appear below the infirmary window
with his hand in a pile of other people's plums.
At times like these he thought to do the should:
contemplating levity, alleviating situations,
the mundanity of actual mystics' revels.
And what it was whosoever this was found
was that the notion of dispensing magnanimity
lingered when the deed was finished in his mind.
The thinking of it filled up other thoughts.
God became the gangrene and the healing
and the nurse cleaning up and the chamber pot.
So returning to the other scene, we find our hero
skipping charcoal briquettes across an evening pond
when Bobby comes and almost pushes him in the water.
"I just saved your life," he says as he pulls him back.
Later, Hank is writing his resignation letter
on the coffee table where his answering machine rests.
Over thirty messages have been sent to him from mothers
who couldn't heat their babies' bottles and nursing homes
at wit's end without Hank's clean-burning, efficient gas.

So Hank repents of his misanthropic wrath, and marshals
all his friends to deliver tanks after Buck's new boy
drove all the HAZMAT drivers to quit. Thus Arlen
is warm, and Hank has reestablished his dharmic path,
though if I called it that he would probably kick my ass.
I would it were such moments weren't condensed
from miasmal banalities and joy uncontingient.
I would it were it didn't take so long to get Bobby's joke.
But as I began this poem (everything before now came later),
I was sitting substitute at a desk at an elementary school,
proctoring fifth graders as they finished up a reading quiz.
Having lingered in ennui for several days, I realized then
I could have been the woman who designed the Sterilite
3-Door Organizer, which is not considered beautiful
only because it was carved from petroleum and not
red cedar or silver maple, or camphor, or cherry wood.
But now all I can think of is the final shot of the show:
Bobby twists the steering wheel of the tow truck
Hank has rigged to skirt around the HAZMAT laws.
"Saved your life!" he says again. Hank finally laughs.

Meditation at the Great Channels

All things fall and are built again
And those that build them again are gay.
　　　—Yeats, "Lapis Lazuli"

I
There is an archipelago of mountain towns,
almost unmapped, hidden between the big roads,
in strips of green on the bacon of the map,
where once there used to be a woodwrought world.

Sailing north from Saltville (north-northwest)
deciduous trees give way to veins of pine,
sumac torches tapering their flames
showing where much grows, but little is grown.

The settlers here have called the land Poor Valley,
contrasting with Rich Valley to the south.
Scottish farm names dominate the later:
Campbell, Clark, Buchanan, Burkett, Brickey.

Kestner, though, a solid German name,
fits better Hayter's Gap, a few miles beyond.
These have the feel of facts, but who could know?
The catalogue is twisted, fragmentary.

Still, this Hayter's Gap. It isn't quite a town.
Maybe hinterland would be a better word,
describing here the port behind a sea
and not that other something it has meant.

Low, exposed, below the cattle line
(the land can take their nibbling, if not crops)
the ground's a pale green, tufted by the foam
of limestone breakers in the painted waves of hills.

Herefords converge on pipe rail rings in winter;
white sun motes crack against the frostburnt earth.
Route 80 limns between Saltville and the Channels.
Jack Kestner is the place's foremost son.

II
Jack Kestner was a man of broad degree
who wrote of war and dogs and hummingbirds;
a widower, who nearing middle age,
returned to his ancestral imprint in the hills
near Hayter's Gap, Clinch Mountain;
who then, exiled from former exiles,
took to writing quietly, deliberately,
of all indeliberate elemental things.

He had been, once, a swinger after birches,
before the guild of Hemingway in him called,
and from the sigodlin plow he went forth unwavering
to New Orleans, Bermuda, Newport News,
wherever the terse earth of fact
(bluetinted, wet) suggested.

For twenty years, around God's great blue earth,
Jack Kestner saw important things and said them artfully,
which was the first and only craft of journalism.

In Antarctica and New Zealand,
throughout the world with expeditional tenseness,
Kestner reported on military procedures
and administrations. Once, he almost broke
the Cuban Missile Crisis, before better judgment
caused him to retract. He traveled almost everywhere,
doing all a real reporter could be asked to do.

But then, peradventure glutted with adventures,
or with the ennui of exteriors (one coworker's body
has bursten early, and a wife's), Kestner
took two children and retired early
to a cabin in the mountains of Virginia.

So for twenty other years of mountain work,
the memory's phlegmatic wiring wavered in him weekly,
favoring at times varieties of hibernating fuzz,
at times the dense polemic. Or memories.

Returning to his source, Jack Kestner
wrote of that first source and his adventures;
about the loyalty of dogs; the work of tree farms;
and sometimes, of the fire tower
near the Great Channels of Virginia,
on top of Brumley Mountain, above his gap.

III
In his youth, he'd worked there many hours,
gazing with eagle urgency over the crooked mountains
of Virginia, Carolina, and Tennessee.

For weeks, as he wrote, he lived in a cabin
the size of a modest toolshed, watched for fires
and explored the lichened canyons

of Devonian sandstone. At night,
he said of a later returning adventure,
the view went on for almost sixty miles.

His station is abandoned now, of course.
The cabin where he used to stay is shorn,
its driftwood eroded by hand and time and wind.

Epithets and initials and drawings of body parts
line the walls against which, once, Kestner's hands
went feeling in the dark to find the door.

All that's stood up are old watch guards' initials
fingered in the concrete with a date.
Even the tower's stairs have been chopped off.

And yet, when things that aren't here now
(entire nations, species, eons and the concepts of them)
had not yet been, this place was already formed.

Perhaps as cricket song, reduced to human speed,
proportioning a cricket's life to ours,
sounds to subjective ears like symphony,

the fungi's marks are tools of conversation,
hieroglyphs the rocks pass to each other,
each letter a remembered mastodon.

IV

I feel an ache for every ancestor.
Beyond the ache of others, I'm not sure, and yet
the aching for them has become my work.

I have been chasing them for so long now,
into a world of hard font Farm Bureau calendars,
the smell of tobacco spit congealing onto concrete floors,
sweat in trucker caps, hard cornered Ford F150s
and women in shoulder pads, with plastic
pearl necklaces and large lensed glasses,

where the news reports are fuzzy
and the river of the microphone drones soft
against the echo of the interviewed expert,
speaking of Chechnya or West Berlin
or Tehran, Iran, or Los Angeles.

I have been chasing them for so long now
that these tattered photographs of words are all I have,
all I have to show myself of the faces they had
before the dismantling of their world. When I come
to the door of their names, I must retreat.

> Jack Kestner,
> Suzie Troxell,
> JoAnn Asbury
>
> Jim Wayne Miller,
> Billy Cuddy,
> Jeanette Bays
>
> Nevada Alison,
> Nevada Stephenson,
> Lou Crabtree
>
> Gene Prater,
> Hobart Smith,
> the cloud of witness:

When I reach them I will know where I am going.

V
I had a dream once, this is real,
where I was lifted in a shaft of light
toward some distant station in the stars,

one of the northern sky's fine constellations,
which name or which significance I'm still not sure.
The Pleiades, I think, has the closest shape.

I felt my body's separations separating.
I knew I should want to want that, but I shuddered,
and the closer to the stars I got, the more I did.

I felt that I would see the face of God,
lie consumed before the aspect of his Grace
if I were not to disengage from this.

I'd like to say I went on, but that's not true.
I felt afraid, and fell out of my dream.
I did not see the face of Jesus,

or the dead, that night nor any night;
not on any mountaintop, nor anywhere.
I am the only souvenir of any pilgrimage I've made.

I'd like to tell you what the dead tell me
in secret conversations. But I can't.
I've stopped expecting conversations with the dead.

I sense a certain shaping in my life.
Maybe that's them. Maybe the doors,
when I feel them close on fiery rooms before I enter,

they have done that. Or maybe there was no fire.
Or maybe I remember things they said
and close the door myself with the hand they gave me.

For now, I know the dead are meaningful.
I know the dead aren't dead, but we don't talk.
I find the face of God in neighbors' faces.

*

There is no one line in the tangled mesh of us.
The past is never fully over, or even fully threshed here,
where the general trend is not so very general.

Living somewhere others had another purpose for
is a delicate, sometimes debilitating, art.
Looking out from the fire tower of my mind,

I see places all around me smoldering,
a ragged architecture of souls
unaware of their own inestimable worth.

So we're not well heeled, and we never will be?
So the company your Daddy worked is as dead as your Daddy?
So the dead don't tell you how to tie a bow on things?

If you believe in prophecies,
you don't stand on Mt. Canaan,
waiting there for God to give commands.

Moses did his work, but now
you have yours, and there's no time
to linger in transfigurations.

All earth is coagulated light,
everything God speaking languages
though the tower stair's without a bottom rung.

Initials on the mountain testify
that some like us have heard the voice before,
and come back home, alive to tell the tale.

Jack Kestner's Brumley Mountain fire tower stands
on sandstone channels older than mankind.
The trail we make was made before we knew.

Matt Prater is a poet and writer from Saltville, VA. Winner of both the George Scarbrough Prize for Poetry and the James Still Prize for Short Story, his work has appeared in a number of journals both regionally (Appalachian Heritage, drafthorse, James Dickey Review, The Hollins Critic, Motif, Now & Then, Still, and Town Creek Poetry) and internationally (The Honest Ulsterman, The Moth, Munyori Literary Journal). He is currently an MFA candidate in poetry at Virginia Tech.

www.ingramcontent.com/pod-product-compliance
Lightning Source LLC
Chambersburg PA
CBHW060227050426
42446CB00013B/3201